AMAZING SCIENCE

AMAZING FORCES AND MOVEMENT

Sally Hewitt

 Crabtree Publishing Company
www.crabtreebooks.com

Crabtree Publishing Company
www.crabtreebooks.com

Editors: L. Michelle Nielsen, Michael Hodge
Senior Editor: Joyce Bentley
Senior Design Manager: Rosamund Saunders
Designer: Tall Tree

Photo Credits: Florida Images/Alamy: p. 17; Leslie Garland Picture Library/Alamy: p. 24; Corbis: p. 7; Randy Faris/Corbis: p. 20; Bill Ross/Corbis: p. 14; Hubert Stadler/Corbis: p. 27; Digital Stock: p. 6; Altrendo Images/Getty Images: p. 8; Phil Banko/Getty Images: p. 15; Andy Crawford/Getty Images: p. 25; Didier Givois/Getty Images: p. 11; David Madison/ Getty Images: p. 10; Ray Massey/ Getty Images: p. 16; Joe McBride/Getty Images: p. 22; Shogoro/ Getty Images: p. 23; Brooke Slezak/ Getty Images: p. 9; Southern Stock/Getty Images p. 13; Steffen Thalemann/ Getty Images: p. 19; Alan Thornton; Getty Images: cover, p. 12; Simon Watson/ Getty Images: p. 21; A T Willet/ Getty Images p. 3, p. 26; David Woolley/ Getty Images: p. 18.

Activity & illustrations: Shakespeare Squared pp. 28-29.

Cover: Athletes race across the finish line.

Title page: A tornado touches down with great force.

Library and Archives Canada Cataloguing in Publication

Hewitt, Sally, 1949-
 Amazing forces and movement / Sally Hewitt.

(Amazing science)
Includes index.
ISBN 978-0-7787-3611-0 (bound)
ISBN 978-0-7787-3625-7 (pbk.)

 1. Force and energy--Juvenile literature. 2. Motion--Juvenile literature. I. Title. II. Series: Hewitt, Sally, 1949- . Amazing science.

QC73.4.H49 2007   j531'.6   C2007-904306-2

Library of Congress Cataloging-in-Publication Data

Hewitt, Sally, 1949-
 Amazing forces and movement / Sally Hewitt.
  p. cm. -- (Amazing science)
 Includes index.
 ISBN-13: 978-0-7787-3611-0 (rlb)
 ISBN-10: 0-7787-3611-3 (rlb)
 ISBN-13: 978-0-7787-3625-7 (pb)
 ISBN-10: 0-7787-3625-3 (pb)
 1. Force and energy--Juvenile literature. I. Title. II. Series.

 QC73.4.H372 2006
 531'.6--dc22

                                        2007027424

Crabtree Publishing Company
www.crabtreebooks.com   1-800-387-7650

Printed in the U.S.A./112010/AL20101101

Published in Canada
Crabtree Publishing
616 Welland Ave.
St. Catharines, ON
L2M 5V6

Published in the United States
Crabtree Publishing
PMB 59051
350 Fifth Avenue, 59ᵗʰ Floor
New York, New York 10118

Published by CRABTREE PUBLISHING COMPANY
Copyright © **2008**

Contents

Amazing forces

...5, 4, 3, 2, 1, blast off!
A huge blast **pushes** a
rocket away from
Earth out into space.

A **force** is a push or a **pull** that makes things move.

A push or a pull can make things move up, down, backward, forward, or around and around.

A man is pushing his daughter on a swing.

YOUR TURN!

Make a ball and a toy car move in different ways. Did you give each a push or a pull?

SCIENCE WORDS: force   move

Push and pull

A snowplow is a big, powerful machine. It has a strong metal bucket to push and lift enormous loads.

Snowplows move forward and push the snow in front of them.

Pushing is the opposite of pulling. You pull a sled along behind you over the snow.

YOUR TURN!

Put on and take off a pair of gloves. Are you giving them a push, a pull, or both?

A sled moves easily over slippery snow.

SCIENCE WORDS: **push pull**

Moving along

A race car speeds along a track. Its powerful **engine** makes a loud, roaring sound.

The engine makes a strong force that pushes the car forward.

Bikes do not have engines. You have to push the **pedals** to make the **wheels** turn.

YOUR TURN!

What moves along on wheels? What force turns the wheels?

The force of your legs moves the bike.

SCIENCE WORDS: **engine   pedals   wheels**

Running fast

Sprinters are the fastest runners in the world. They need a lot of strength and power to run fast.

Runners have strong **muscles** to power them along.

Muscles pull your bones when you move. Strong muscles help you run faster and jump higher.

Exercise helps build muscles and keep them strong.

SCIENCE WORDS: fast muscles

13

Start and stop

Eurostar is a high speed train. It speeds over the ground and under the sea between London, England, and Paris, France.

The driver uses the controls to **start**, move, and **stop** the train. Trains slow down and stop at train stations.

Computers tell the driver how fast the train is going.

The train speeds along straight tracks and slows down on winding tracks.

SCIENCE WORDS: **start   stop   slow**

Rubbing together

Sharks have **shapes** that helps them swim fast. They are smooth and pointed, which helps them cut through the **water**.

Water and air **rub** against objects that move through them and slow the objects down.

When things rub together, they make a force called **"friction"**. Friction slows things down.

▲ The toy truck's wheels rub against the carpet. It slows down and stops.

SCIENCE WORDS: **rub   friction**

17

Changing shape

Pizza chefs toss, flatten, push, and pull dough. They use their hands to make it into a flat, round shape.

Pushing and pulling squashy, stretchy materials, such as dough, **changes** their shapes.

When you blow air into a balloon, it changes shape.

YOUR TURN!

Push, pull, squash, and stretch modeling clay to make new shapes.

Blowing pushes air into the stretchy balloon.

SCIENCE WORDS: change   shape

Elastic and springs

A bungee jumper dives off of a tall crane. An **elastic** cord stops her **fall** and bounces her back up again.

Elastic material stretches when you pull it. It snaps back into shape when you let it go.

A **spring** in a pogo stick squashes when you push it down.

The spring pushes back up to make the rider bounce.

YOUR TURN!

Push down on a stapler. Let go and watch how the springs inside make it jump open.

SCIENCE WORDS: elastic spring

Falling

A skydiver jumps from an airplane and falls through the air. **Gravity** pulls the skydiver down to the ground.

Things fall down because of a natural force called "gravity".

When a parachute is released, air pushes up on the parachute and slows the skydiver's fall.

YOUR TURN!

Drop a piece of paper. How does it fall? Now crumple it and drop it again. How does it fall now?

A parachute slows a skydiver's fall and stops him or her from hitting the ground too hard.

SCIENCE WORDS: gravity   fall

Magnets

A giant **magnet** on a crane pulls **iron** toward it with a strong force called **"magnetism"**.

Things made of iron are magnetic.
A magnet pulls and moves
magnetic things.

A magnet cannot pick up things
made of plastic, wool, or wood.

YOUR TURN!

*Collect things made
of metal, plastic, and wood.
Use a magnet. What will it
pull, move, and pick up?*

Metal paperclips
stick to a magnet.

SCIENCE WORDS: magnet iron magnetism

25

Wind and water

A tornado is a swirling tube of **wind**. It is strong enough to knock down large buildings and houses.

Wind is moving air. You can feel it pushing against you.

Flowing water is a strong force. It pushes against things and moves them along.

YOUR TURN!

Fly a kite. Feel the wind push it up in the air.

The force of water pushes a water wheel around.

SCIENCE WORDS: **wind   water**

Seeing invisible forces

Watch what happens to the iron filings when they are placed around a magnet.

What you need

- bar magnet
- paper
- blank transparency
- pencil
- iron filings

1. Place the bar magnet flat on a desk. Make sure that it is in the middle of the desk.

2. Have a partner hold the transparency just above the magnet. Make sure that your partner holds it steady.

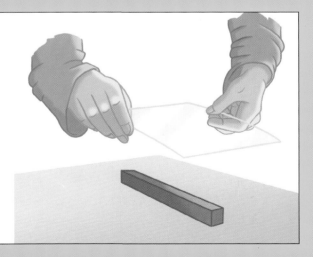

3. Sprinkle the iron filings onto the transparency above the bar magnet.

4. Give the transparency several light taps with your finger. Pay close attention to what happens to the iron filings. Draw what you see on a piece of paper.

What you will see:

As you tap the transparency you should see the iron filings move into lines. Why? These lines show the forces that surround a magnet. By carefully looking at the lines formed by the filings, you can see both poles (where many filings have drifted) and the neutral center of the magnet (where there are few or no filings).

Glossary

change   When you change something, you make it different.

elastic   Elastic stretches when you pull it and snaps back when you let it go.

engine   An engine gives cars, tractors, trains, and airplanes the power that they need to move.

fall   An object will fall down when you drop it.

fast   Moving fast is moving very quickly. It is the opposite of slow.

force   A force is a push or a pull that makes things move.

friction   When things rub together, they make a force called "friction".

gravity   Gravity is a force that pulls things down towards the ground.

iron   Iron is a kind of metal.

magnet   A magnet pulls things made of iron toward it with a force called "magnetism".

magnetism   A natural force. A magnet pulls metal objects toward it with magnetism.

move   When you move, you are not still. Pushes and pulls make things move.

muscles Your muscles push and pull your bones when you move.

pedals You push pedals on a bike to turn the wheels and make the bike move.

pull You pull something toward you to make it move or change shape.

push You push something away from you to make it move or change shape.

rub You rub a mirror with a cloth to clean it. You rub your hands together to make them warm.

shape The outline of an object. A ball has a round shape. A snake has a long, thin shape.

slow Not moving quickly. Slow is the opposite of fast.

spring A spring is a coil that squashes when you push down on it and springs back up when you let it go.

start To start is to begin. Something starts to move when it is given a push or a pull.

stop To stop moving is to be still.

water Flowing water is a force that can make things move.

wheels A wheel is round. Cars and trucks move along on turning wheels.

wind Wind is moving air.

Index